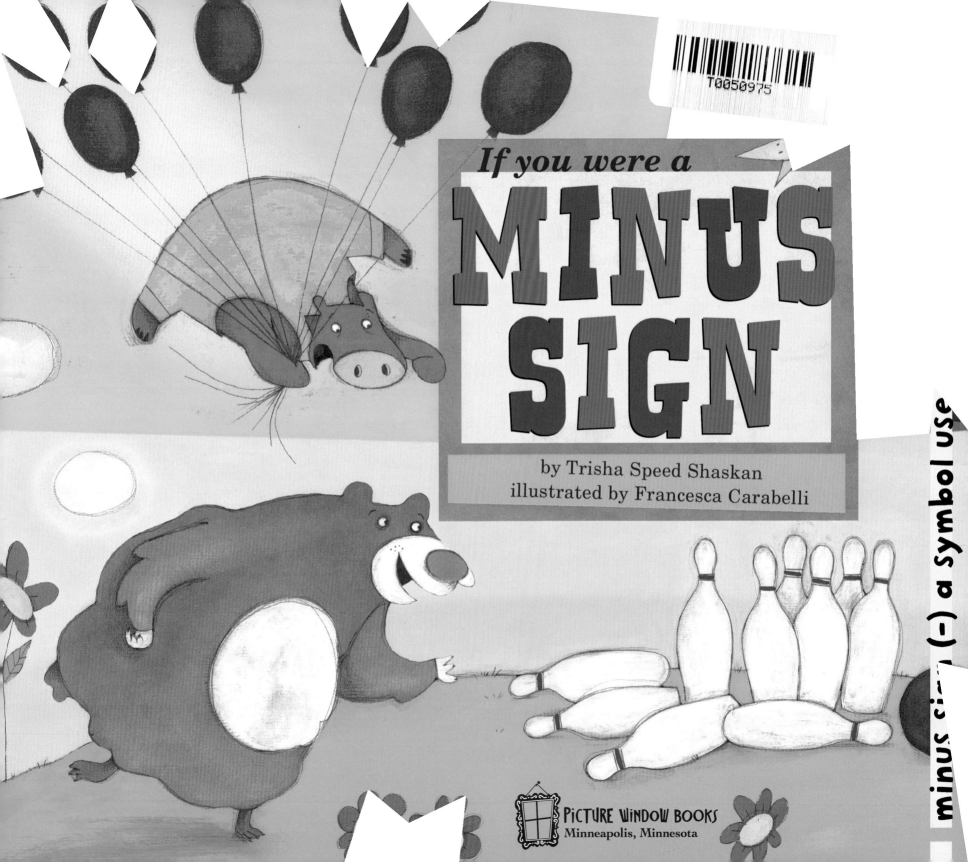

If you were a MINUS SIGN

by Trisha Speed Shaskan

illustrated by Francesca Carabelli

PICTURE WINDOW BOOKS
Minneapolis, Minnesota

minus sign (–) a symbol use

Editor: Christianne Jones
Designers: Nathan Gassman and Hilary Wacholz
Page Production: Melissa Kes
The illustrations in this book were created with acrylics.

Picture Window Books
A Capstone Imprint
1710 Roe Cresst Drive
North Mankato, MN 56003
www.capstonepub.com

Special thanks to our advisers for their expertise:

Stuart Farm, M.Ed., Mathematics Lecturer, University of North Dakota

Terry Flaherty, Ph.D., Professor of English, Minnesota State University, Mankato

Library of Congress Cataloging-in-Publication Data
Shaskan, Trisha Speed, 1973-
If you were a minus sign / by Trisha Speed Shaskan ; illustrated by Francesca Carabelli.
p. cm. — (Math fun)
Includes index.
ISBN 978-1-4048-4787-3 (library binding)
ISBN 978-1-4048-4788-0 (paperback)
1. Mathematical notation—Juvenile literature. 2. Subtraction—Juvenile literature.
I. Carabelli, Francesca, ill. II. Title.
QA41.S48 2009
513.2'12—dc22   2008006457

Printed in the United States   5989

If you were a minus sign ...

... you would subtract one number from another.

Hugo has twelve balloons.

A bird bursts six of Hugo's balloons.
Hugo has six balloons left.

$$\begin{array}{r} 12 \\ -\ 6 \\ \hline 6 \end{array}$$

If you were a minus sign, you would be a symbol used to show subtraction. You would be part of a subtraction problem.

Starry-eyed Stella's daisy has nine petals.
Stella plucks eight petals from it.
Stella's daisy has one petal left.

7

If you were a minus sign, you would be used in place of the words "take away."

Mama Munk finds twelve acorns.
She takes away five to hide.
Twelve take away five is seven.
Seven acorns are left.

$$\begin{array}{r} 12 \\ -\ 5 \\ \hline 7 \end{array}$$

Papa Munk finds seven acorns.
He takes away five to hide.
Seven take away five is two.
Two acorns are left.

$$7 - 5 = 2$$

If you were a minus sign, you would help show the difference in a subtraction problem.

$$10 - 4 \over 6$$

There are ten bowling pins. Bruno knocks down four of them. Six bowling pins are left standing. The difference between ten and four is six.

If you were a minus sign, you could work left to right or top to bottom.

Patty fries seven burgers. She puts five on a plate. Two are left in the pan.

7 - 5 = 2

Patty stacks seven burgers.
She serves two and has five left.

$$\begin{array}{r} 7 \\ -\,2 \\ \hline 5 \end{array}$$

If you were a minus sign, you could help solve a story problem.

14

$$\begin{array}{r} 11 \\ -4 \\ \hline 7 \end{array}$$

Sandy blew eleven bubbles.
Gill popped four of them.
How many bubbles were left?
Eleven minus four equals seven.
Seven bubbles were left.

If you were a minus sign, you could subtract small numbers.

There are nine glasses of fruit punch on the table. Three thirsty tigers take three glasses away. There are six left.

$$9 - 3 = 6$$

There are twenty-four pieces of pizza. Some hungry hippos take ten pieces away. There are fourteen left.

$$\begin{array}{r} 24 \\ -10 \\ \hline 14 \end{array}$$

If you were a minus sign, you could subtract big numbers.

There are 120 cupcakes on the cupcake tree.
Some lunching lizards take 100 cupcakes away.
There are 20 cupcakes left.

$$120 - 100 = 20$$

Mama and Papa Potbelly pop 1,500 pieces of corn. The Potbelly family eats 1,000 pieces of popcorn. There are 500 pieces left.

$$\begin{array}{r} 1,500 \\ -\ 1,000 \\ \hline 500 \end{array}$$

If you were a minus sign, you would be part of a subtraction problem. You could use addition to check the answer to your subtraction problem.

Jack pulls seven doves out of his hat. He makes five disappear. Jack is left with two doves.

$$7 - 5 = 2$$

To check your answer, add the five birds that have disappeared to the two in the hat. You have seven birds.

$$5 + 2 = 7$$

You would always subtract one number from another ...

... if you were a minus sign.

Jump into SUBTRACTION

Using sidewalk chalk, draw a large number line. A number line looks like a ruler. Then draw marks on it for each number. Write the numbers in order from one to ten. Leave enough space between each number to jump from one to the next. Now, it's time to subtract.

1. Start on the number ten. Jump three numbers down the line toward the number one. The number you landed on is the difference between ten and three. 10-3=?

2. Start on the number eight. Jump four numbers down the line toward number one. The number you landed on is the difference between eight and four. 8-4=?

3. Start on the number seven. Jump three numbers down the line toward number one. The number you landed on is the difference between seven and three. 7-3=?

Now make up at least five subtraction problems of your own. Solve them by jumping down the number line!

1 2 3 4 5 6 7 8 9 10

Answers: 1. (7) 2. (4) 3. (4)

23

Glossary

difference—the number left after subtracting one number from another

minus sign—a symbol used to show subtraction

subtract—to take away one part, or number, from another

subtraction—taking one number from another number

symbol—a sign that stands for something else

To Learn More

More Books to Read

Cleary, Brian P. *The Action of Subtraction*. Minneapolis: Millbrook Press, 2006.

Franco, Betsy. *Subtraction Fun*. Mankato, Minn.: Yellow Umbrella Books, 2002.

Leedy, Loreen. *Subtraction Action*. New York: Holiday House, 2002.

On the Web

FactHound offers a safe, fun way to find Web sites related to topics in this book. All of the sites on FactHound have been researched by our staff.

1. Visit *www.facthound.com*
2. Type in this special code: 1404847871
3. Click on the FETCH IT button.

Your trusty FactHound will fetch the best sites for you!

Look for all of the books in the Math Fun series

If You Were a Fraction

If You Were a Minus Sign

If You Were a Plus Sign

If You Were a Set

If You Were an Even Number

If You Were an Odd Number